The Good Green Footstool

The Good Green Footstool

Florence Becker Lennon

Westview Press • Boulder, Colorado

Some of these poems have appeared in the following publications: *Colorado Daily, Colorado Quarterly, Ecologos, Literary Review, Southwest, Tomorrow, Town & Country Review* (Boulder, Colorado), and F. P. Adams's column "Conning Tower," in the New York *World.*

Copyright 1976 by Florence Becker Lennon.

Published 1976 in the United States of America by

Westview Press, Inc.
1898 Flatiron Court
Boulder, Colorado 80301
Frederick A. Praeger, Publisher and Editorial Director

Library of Congress Cataloging in Publication Data

Lennon, Florence Becker.
    The good green footstool.

    I. Title.
PS3523.E563G6   811'.5'2   76-5428
ISBN 0-89158-046-8

Printed and bound in the United States of America.

Cover and dust jacket by Eleonore Blaurock-Busch.
Frontispiece by Rob Pudim.
Photo of the author by Phil Stern.

for Carl

Contents

Outsight 1

The Good Green Footstool
Come Down
October Storm — Aftermath
Our Town
Escape from Pavement
Desert Island
Voice for the Wilderness
Cassandra Says
Whitman Montage
Mountain City
Ah, Wilderness!
The Triumph of DDT
In Orbit
Homage to Sir Isaac
Celestial Visitor
Landscape with Figures
To All My Darling Young Friends (of Fifty and Under) Especially
Joe Sullivan in Majorca
Global Housekeeping
Scene Before
"Serpent!" Cried the Wood Pigeon
Very Funny
Please!
Co-existence
Good Neighbor
To Earth, with Love

Insight 29

Gradus Ad Parnassum
Typographic Poem
Poetry for the Ear
Poetry Festival
The Poet's Task
The Uses of Poetry
Visit to an Atelier
Music from Above
Moving from Pen to Paint
Remembering Robert Frost

Clear Sight   43

Scaring Myself
Ancestral Voices Crying
Go Away Gabriel
Relief
Sonnets of Loss: **I** Memorial   **II** The Second Coming
III The Unfinished Symphony of Helen Tamiris
Dithyrambos
The Silent Piano
P.S. to Housman's *Reveille*
The Lure
Terminal Sonnets: **I** La Ronde   **II** Nevertheless

Near Sight   57

Women's Lib
They Say: He Says   She Says
Message from the Witch's Ashes
Bittersweet: Bitter   Sweet   Bittersweet
Psyche, 1923
I How Do I Love Thee? 1925   **II** How Do I Love Thee? 1963
III How Do I Love Thee? 1970
Unbirthday Card for a Distant Beloved 1971

Hindsight   67

Birthright
No Choice
Incommunicado
Hostages to Fortune
La Plus Belle Femme
Blessing
Tao
Socrates 1970
Irrelevant
Almost April
Montessori School

Late Sight   81

Love Story
City Delicatessen
A Little Late
Passover House

The Truth
Reach Out
Don't Fence Me In
Are You There?
Generation Gap

Far Sight   93

Prayer for Our Time
The Next Step
Another Chapter
Invocation at Delphi
Gonna Play on My Harp
The Woodchopper of Doorn or How History Repeats Itself
Late American
Oil's Well: I —And John (D) is His Prophet (ca. 1926)
II Habeas Corpus (ca. 1929) III John the Baptist (ca. 1934)
Lorelei
Epitaph for Ozymandias
My Lie
Indispensable Man   A Montage

More Light   111

The Lesson for Today
Have We?
In Whose Footsteps?
Leaden Lining
Kol Nidrei
Oi, Oi, Oi
They Have Us in the Earth
A Sort of Prayer during a Heat Wave and After Reading
Martin Buber

Outsight

The Good Green Footstool

O Lord, good Lord,
give me the footstool—
You take the throne.
I want the footstool—
the good green footstool—
give me the footstool, Lord—
You keep the throne.

Come Down

Have no hubris, be not proud
that you can poke a hole in cloud:
through that hole can leak the ray
that cloud was meant to keep away.

October Storm — Aftermath

The weeping birch took many months to die.
Catalpa, maple, broke big branches, froze
their fingers only. Birch and willow lie
cut corpses, for exploding ice arrows
within the trunks had broken both their hearts.
Spring leaves came out, and it was June before
they browned and curled. The willow made new starts
of supple shoots. The birch could sprout no more.
I mourn, and swear to wrap all trunks this fall,
add mulch, straw, fertilizer. Who could guess
October snow would drop a heavy pall,
drown leaves, freeze hearts, crash massive limbs with stress?
Perhaps we hung that curtain in the air
composed of trash we have been sending there?

Our Town

Tumbleweed straggles on the railroad track
where children balance safely on the rail;
the interstate blots out the cattle trail,
a sulphur flag waves from the giant stack.
The houses crawling up the mountain lack
deep roots—may they not slide into the vale!
And—can you tell the schoolhouse from the jail?
(No mountain windows—each a solid back.)

You never really were a peaceful town—
snatched from the Indians for the greed of gold,
hard against unions, with a burning cross,
hooded and sheeted against black and brown.
Your errors are impossible to gloss,
nor will your beauty abdicate its hold.

Escape from Pavement

I could kiss the dusty road before my door.
Dear dusty road—the snake inscribes his monogram,
the quail imprint their feet, raccoons their pads,
ten thousand tiny ants draw a straight line,
the butterfly gone still, the caterpillar humping—
here's all the news in print.

Desert Island

Goodbye Manhattan, you have been my nurse
and cruel stepmother. My father bought
and sold your plots; perhaps he really thought
the sun set in the Hudson. Even worse,
we never saw the sea. Who laid the curse
that turned you all to stone and steel? The taut
sharp faces show that all of us are caught—
another year, and I would leave you in a hearse.

Pardon this rudeness to my native town,
where I was schooled, that holds my oldest friends—
but still—the monster buildings knock me down
and ride upon my chest. How can I make amends?
There are no window-sills—the birds are gone—
and I must follow, or my story ends.

Voice for the Wilderness

The house, no longer silent, pulses, roars,
cleans, freezes, heats, distributes with a fan,
miscarries refuse to the sea. Prodigal man
drives suds into the springs, lightens his chores
by ruining his home, plundering the stores,
laid by so slowly since the earth began,
to feed his whizzing, clanking caravan.
Turning his back on sun and all outdoors
he stares at shadows dancing on the wall
or rides on ribbon roads from here to there
noticing nothing, forfeiting the feel
of foot on earth, the smell of country air,
the gift of silence, and the robin's call.
Perhaps we ought to disinvent the wheel.

Cassandra Says

Buildings should rise no higher than a tree;
houses of worship at sequoia height
need not offend, if pointed to the light,
as the sequoias are. Does mankind need to be
piled high in heavy boxes? Who is free
living with doors and windows sealed up tight,
riding hydraulic coffins day and night,
a prisoner's patch of sky all he can see?

Box Canyon threatens to erupt
a forest of aluminum and glass
Towers of Babel bring us up abrupt,
block the horizon—windows wink and glare
across the street bereft of trees, of grass,
of flowers, birds, of sun and moon—and air.

Whitman Montage

Where is your city, Walt?
City nested in bays, fish-shaped Paumanok?
Slobbered with creeping concrete;
Castle Garden gone, Brooklyn Ferry gone,
the manly race of drivers of horses gone.

Million-footed Manhattan staggers down subway stairs;
smartly attired, countenance smiling, form upright,
depth under the breast-bone, hell under the skull-bones,
speaking of anything else, but never of itself.

We can hardly hear your call to battle, Walt:
I nourish active rebellion;
not a grave of the lover of freedom but grows seeds for
        freedom.

Oh hasten flag of man
Turn, o Libertad.

Where are you, Libertad?
Fled down the open road, the slowly closing.

Mountain City

No sooner did the earth erect a fold
above the slow sweep to the river
than Thunderbird, black feathers flashing,
settled his nest on the far side.

Today the dwellers in the city
gaze at the mountain for their weather.
They know when Thunderbird begins to tremble.
Then the celestial zoo tears loose;
then they abandon further traffic
settle on the west verandahs to behold
blue panthers lunging in the skies,
their zigzag talons harboring hot murder,
rolling down the mountain full of anger,
down the river's slow meander.

Thunderbird grumbles again behind the mountain,
amber flamingos dance over the canyon,
lose their ardor, wander farther from the valley.

Thunderbird, still brooding,
finds time to dissemble the end of the fandango—
then suddenly soars, clutching the orange serpent in his
        beak,
releasing him with a terrific bang
and drops behind the mountain till another day.

Ah, Wilderness!
(For Joseph Wood Krutch)

Grand Canyon is a place of prayer
except when planes explode the air
but—those are people way up there;

they want to see the Canyon too.
They see it more indeed than you
who pluck a pebble from your shoe

and plod along the southern rim
to watch the orange slowly dim
and purple rise right to the brim

while moonlight shifts the shapes around.
Until the final plane is downed
where there are sights there will be sound.

The Triumph of DDT

In what year will it happen
that the sky will be empty of angel wings all day
while devil wings flap from dusk to dawn?

What little brown brother bat
will take over the mission of insect eater and maker of
        guano,
and who, oh who, will lift the heart of man,
lacking the bluebird, the cardinal,
the junco, and the solemn owl?

On the first day of that year
let me go down with the birds.

In Orbit

I first came awake in the brightness before the spring
on a sky-blue, sun-yellow morning between the snows.
Like Hiawatha, I am born again:
already at the Winter solstice something stirs
with the first beginning of buds.

Likewise the death of summer begins with its birth
as the sun slides down the ecliptic.
Even in June the darkness comes sooner day by day
and I cannot forget the coming of winter.

Homage to Sir Isaac

Behold the common enemy:
entropy, gravity,
inertia—form the trinity.

Celestial Visitor

The comet has a quaint idea:
instead of coming every year
until he grows banal, like spring,
he makes elliptic journeying
more calculated to surprise
and focus all the yokels' eyes
upon the old familiar sky
that he lights up in passing by.

Landscape with Figures

We have to trim the cottonwoods
else they drop their tired limbs on our heads.
Twenty feet up their leaves waggle
like their cousins', the aspens.

The bike trail begins by the library
runs under cottonwoods, over the bridge.
That is all the old lady sees of the trail;
it is fifty years since she pedalled a bike.
She is happy not to fall off her feet,
happy the bikes don't knock her down.
And that the kids say "Hi!"

To All My Darling Young Friends
(of Fifty and Under)
Especially Joe Sullivan in Majorca

Try to think of me as a bad old baby
grabbing for a piece of the moon
before it sets.

I was a revolutionist?
A demonstrator—picketer—leafletter?
An atheist (we say humanist now), a free lover?
Look again!
A Greenwich Village grandmother
in a danse macabre.

O.K. kids.
Grandma has sat down;
she wants to hear those last poems
thumping and knocking to get out.
Now you have permission to wipe your own noses;
Grandma's busy.

Global Housekeeping

Throw, throw, throw away:
Trash won't go away—
There is no away—

But

Through the concrete the crocus pushes—
(Will there be water if we probe?)

Or

Plant Mt. Plastic with kleenex bushes
and girdle with garbage the globe?

Scene Before

Here come the smiling villains
with their golden calf:
they want your house, your farm,
your quiet street, your little shop.
They will give you paper
exchangeable for metal (it says here),
exchangeable for X.

I have seen a pushcart full of paper
that would not buy a postage stamp.

Go ahead—sell your house
and count the change.

What becomes of the house?
A parking lot—what else?

"Serpent!" Cried the Wood Pigeon

How must I look to a bird?
My eyes are as big as his head.

The brave ones snatch seeds ten feet from my chair;
suppose I pounce?
Nor is my record pure.
Perhaps their spies have told them
about the Thanksgiving turkey
and the breakfast egg.

Very Funny

In this nice new lemming world
where snowmobile screeches to snowmobile in the
        former wilderness
and trailer home nudges trailer home over the prairie dog
        colony,
while the Audubon Society recycles the prairie dogs out
        by the reservoir;
where we plant flags on the moon,
dig holes in the Van Allen belt
rig offices in the stratosphere—

where does one go now for a weekend at Walden?

Please!

Oh bear with the bear
share with the bear
be fair to the bear:
we need him.

We need not feed him—
he finds his own
on bush, under stone.

If the grizzly leaves us
he bereaves us.

O wonder bear
oh blunder bear
sometimes you tear
and murder what you will not eat:
sometimes you laugh, and dance on heavy feet.

You brother bear
you other bear
great man must dare
to let you share
the earth and air
(concrete and glass)
for if you pass
man is the most atrocious
most ferocious
bear.

Co-existence

Dear St. Francis

What must I do about raccoons?
The neighbors seem to give them a bad name:
they gang up on our cats and dogs to kill
they scoop the goldfish from the lily pool
they scratch and even bite the human hand
they carry rabies.
It may be so.

They wear a question on their faces
they never foul their feeding places
they bring such gaiety to my patio
they have such fluffy babies
they troop in like a robber band
play Harlequin and Columbine and Fool
hang from the vine, peer in the window, mill,
scuffle, importune, pray—who wants them tame?
Please, may I feed the naughty pantaloons,
Dear St. Francis?

Good Neighbor

My neighbor the meadowlark
makes his nest in a field,
perches on a utility pole
sings a passage from the Pastorale;
he is one of the few birds who responds
to my response.
We had long conversations.

We used to think birds sang
only for love or joy.
Now we know they also sing to say
"This is my space—please go away."

Oh to be a bird—
to make war with song.

To Earth, with Love
(Villanelle)

Have patience, dear green planet—stay a while:
my grandchildren will befriend you.
Hold roots and rivers in your ancient style;

let not the menacing atomic pile
from your proper orbit send you—
have patience, dear green planet—stay a while.

Ignore the ignorant who would defile,
reject the enemies who rend you:
hold roots and rivers in your ancient style.

Trust us who love you, give us your green smile:
reward your lovers who defend you—
have patience, dear green planet, stay a while.

Though the smog curtain hangs above a mile,
gently the lovely young will mend you:
hold roots and rivers in your ancient style.

Granted we deserve exile—
evil we did not intend you.
Have patience, dear green planet—stay a while,
hold roots and rivers in your ancient style.

Insight

Gradus Ad Parnassum

The poet sat in Washington Square
groping for poems that never came
savagely doodling Apollo's name;
as he looked up, Apollo was there.

The poet muttered, "My words don't sing—
You see, boss, all I learned before
suddenly doesn't fit any more—
the Einstein equation changed everything.

I've tried fractured syntax and four-letter words
Words—you know the juggling I've done with 'em—
I've slanted my rhyme and sprung my rhythm—
modern poetry's for the birds!

Poets and listeners are confused.
English won't do it and neither will Greek—
there has to be a new technique."
Apollo answered, "I too have mused . . .

Your problem is mainly a matter of time."
He vanished. The poet, with frantic stare,
threw a handy rope ladder into the air,
and slowly, clumsily, started to climb.

Typographic Poem

e. e. cummings and gertrude stein
from their island universes
emit a beam
that eventually o eventually
will reach this planet
gone cold o cold po
tato

Poetry for the Ear

Homer could not read or write, Shakespeare could not
    spell;
the Trojan war was long before blind Homer came to tell
with voice and lyre and epic fire how Priam's city fell,
and Shakespeare too composed for voice—his own and
    other men's and boys'.

Then poets, learn to sing once more
to chirp, to whistle, and to roar—
to charm the wild life from its den:
the tape recorder, not the pen
the ancient bards' inheritor.

Poetry Festival

I had two glasses of Belgian wine
shook hands with three Russians
drank brotherhood with one Pole
(North or South, I can't recall)
and we all agreed
the greatest living poet—

Robert Burns.

The Poet's Task

A poet is a device
for transmuting light to sound:
he is to think the unthinkable
speak the unspeakable
attempt the impossible
and celebrate each failure
in cadenced verse.

Where is a poem?
In the mushroom's shade
the violet's eye
the listener's ear.

The Uses of Poetry

Morning sun through the window
on my knife, slicing a large onion on a small board
(always be specific)
presents the question: What good is poetry?
And why should poets take up space?

The man said clearly
poets cannot stop the bomb.
Suppose all the poets in the world assembled
singing at the top of their song—
then what? Who listens?

Only the man who invented dynamite
The Field Marshall who was Viceroy of India
The man who "won" the last war
The Emperor of Japan
One President of the United States
and Hobson and Jobson
and you and I.

Visit to an Atelier
(For Miklos Dallos)

The sculptor's hand and eye are almost one:
a form, remembering a woman—
breasts melt into buttocks, marble-soft, and veined—
enough—though not quite human,
but in another figure he retained
all save the head.
It spoils the composition, so he said.

Music from Above

The tall archangel in evening dress
flipped his black tails over the piano bench
breaking into that old drinking song
war song
anthem they call it.
The audience rose,
my two heads snarled at each other.

The archangelic head bent over the piano
as the Appassionata burst and flowed through those
    hands.

Oh archangel—drop that drinking song.

Moving from Pen to Paint

Once the world was all of words.
How godlike—name it, and it was done.
To move from hear and say
to see and show
is night and day.

Within the mind lies a quiet pool
in a forest opening
where birds come to sing.
Sit there and wait
and meditate.
Birds bring a poem.

Sometimes the birds don't come
and you go away.
Sometimes the poem comes when you are busy.
Listen—it won't come back;
you must be ready.

How different is the world of light:
always there.
Listener, learn to look.
Windows open up inside,
the light keeps changing.
Paint all day
come back tomorrow
next year.
It is always there, never twice the same.

Can you paint the Flatirons?
Or Grand Canyon?
Try again.

Remembering Robert Frost

Silent now that rugged voice
but listen:
it resounds within;
the voice of God the Farmer
half Hesiod and half Jahweh,
cognizant of the tides of earth
and of the human heart.

He set us all upon the ground-swell,
tuned our ears to the inner tides;
he heard the outer world as well
and lent his presence to the President
who gave him in return the larger stage.

Jester and sage
majestic simplicity
both oak and vine
deep-rooted, tendrils turning to the light.

To us his gift outright;
the sunwise turn.

Clear Sight

Scaring Myself

The shadow of the hawk recalls
what bides around the corner
and will not show its face.

Carrying the skeleton from the closet
setting it up to draw
looking in its no-eyes, was easy.
It was not my death.
The enemy is within and waits its time.

Worse is the know-not-what.
It lurks to pounce in a dark street
it hums in machinery and thumps in jazz.

When the know-not-what
joins the enemy within
and the noises in the head win out—
what then?

The Dean of St. Paul's
terrorized his congregation
with "The first five minutes after death."
How about the last five minutes before?

Ancestral Voices Crying

Let me say plainly
I am afraid
of all those others in my skin

whose messages arise
deeper than the white whale,
volcanic intrusions from beneath the sea.

Go Away Gabriel

I heard the horn but didn't go;
Gabriel honked, but I stayed home.
Maybe I'll get to greet some great-grandchildren,
maybe even watch them grow.

It's such fun fishing in the gene pool
waiting to see who has blue eyes
who can paint and who has music
who loves people and who loves dogs.

Gabriel, Gabriel, can't you wait?
Haven't you got enough to do?

Relief

One night, as I was paddling down the Nile
in my birch-bark Chipaway canoe,
I heard a splash near my left paddle.

The fractured moon on the water subsided;
the Voice said
there goes another mummy.

The pressure lifted from my chest;
I took a deep breath
and kept on breathing.

Sonnets of Loss

I Memorial
(to Eleanor Roosevelt in the Overseas Press Club)

A bronze plaque on the fire-place spells your name,
and those tough realists, the daily press,
did the unveiling with a light caress
and unshed tears. It will not be the same
at the United Nations. Where you came
was courage, grace, an ear for all distress.
From Wiltwyck to West Pakistan they bless
your memory. Can we place it in a frame?

Weave loss into a banner of world hope,
meet every day with open eyes and heart,
attributing high motives with a smile—
not fooled, but seeking? Like you, can we cope
with villains without villainy? Come—start!
I mean—shall we survive a little while?

II The Second Coming
(for Walter Frankl)

Poets long dead sit on my shelves and sing:
Burns, Byron, Heine, Keats—I hear them all.
The newly dead lie silent. There's a wall
around each one, as if he's listening
to the new grass that covers him, a ring
we cannot cross, and if we try to call
our voices blow away. The grass grows tall
and deep, and silence is a heavy thing.

The roll is long—Aldington, cummings, Frost,
Holmes, Hillyer, Jeffers, Williams and H.D.,
all silenced almost in a single year.
Then, listening for the voices we have lost,
we wait in emptiness and struggle free
and they return upon the inner ear.

III The Unfinished Symphony of Helen Tamiris

This is the pain that will not go away
except I go along. The conqueror
waits quietly, and will not close the door
of death, nor is it any use to pray;
fighting is better. Let nobody say
I quit one battle in my life-long war
against the common enemy, before
his final triumph on my dying day.

I leave my friends a legacy of pride
that from oblivious Manhattan rock
I once like Moses called a living stream
upon whose dancing waves you watched me ride—
and pay, like Moses, with a shattered dream . . .

Dithyrambos

This time Dionysos was reborn a woman
suffered, gave birth, triumphed, and was crucified.

The red scarf, Isadora,
the red scarf about your white throat
snapping your white throat at a moment of ecstatic speed:
the red tendril of the vine that saved the infant Dionysos.
Your youth, your beauty, Isadora,
are preserved to us forever.

Be glad for us, Isadora—
bless the insidious red tendril for our sakes.
You would have been a wise old woman, Isadora—
there are no wise old women.
We needed you to live this life with us,
but it was written:

**DIONYSOS THE NAZARENE SHALL DIE YOUNG
LEAVING A YOUTHFUL IMAGE IN THEIR HEARTS
TO FERTILIZE THE ANNUAL REBIRTH.**

Our daughters shall dance the Dionysia
with your red scarf.

The Silent Piano

There it stands
swallowing its tongue
nobody pressing it to sing.

Fifty years it sang day and night,
humming to itself in the quiet hours.

Now, muffled with an embroidered scarf,
it is a table to hold flowers.

Do ghostly fingers sing it in the night?

P.S. to Housman's *Reveille*

Shall I lie in bed and scold
because the morning is so cold?
Come, old girl, and trot around—
it is much colder in the ground.

The Lure

They are calling me
those who have left us:
the brother and sisters I never knew
the one who lived longer
my parents.

Our unfinished conversations will pull me into the ground.
Or into the furnace smoke;
still I shall not find them.

Terminal Sonnets

I La Ronde

Not death itself, but dying is a bore:
we know quick death can often be a friend,
bringing decay, pain, sorrow, to an end.
My little donkey stumbles, snorts—foot-sore,
impatient, careless—grooming is a chore.
The time is nearly up for us to lend
our borrowed space to one who will defend
our planet from the horrors at the door.

Death of dictators always comes too late,
too slowly their dynasties disappear
and when at last they're added to the earth
still in the wings the new dictators wait;
we bolster up our hope against our fear
while welcome death gives way to welcome birth.

II Nevertheless

The daily miracle has taken place:
I waked this morning to the risen sun
looking for whom to thank, finding no one
in all the starry universe of space.

Oh aging child! When will you learn to face
The Way It Is? All your supports are gone;
we are born alone, and we must die alone,
no one to blame, and worse, no one to praise.

How must we live, how can we slake our thirst?
Give over greed, share power, abandon war
(infant omnipotence, devouring all—
frog that must be a bull, yea though he burst),
spread love, preserve the earth, alone no more
there waits the unborn god—oh heed his call.

Near Sight

Women's Lib

Nurture is woman's nature.
In the garden, pruning plants
in the home, tending children
in the office, taking care of men
or like Indira Gandhi and Golda Meir, nursing a nation:
we must do our thing.

They Say

He Says

Wives of great men all remind us
we can make our wives sublime
keeping them in step behind us
sweeping up the sands of time.

She Says

Each man on his ice-peak
studying the stars
no more hears his wife speak
than if she were on Mars.

Message from the Witch's Ashes

Only Lawrence knew
and he was half a woman
how we wish that men
or one man
would break the broomstick saying
here—try this instead.

Bittersweet

Bitter

It must be fun
to run
to jog, to streak.
I envy you
but haven't the physique.

For some things I can do
(very few)
a partner's needed—please notify if found
other than underground.

Sweet

Well then—the pleasures of the mind:
much easier to find
and limited
only by what is in your head.
The mind contains the whole World's Fair,
all friends and enemies gather there
space-time and evolution spin
the music's on and you are in.

Bittersweet

And yet, until the very end
we crave the wholeness of the blend.

Psyche, 1923

I know love passed me in the night.
There is a perfume in the air,
a feather from his wing,
and it is radiant and white
and I shall wear it in my hair
and sing.

I How Do I Love Thee?   1925

Your head lies on another shoulder now
and on my shoulder lies another head
but I cannot forget how we were wed
one gentle April afternoon, nor how
Jack-in-the-Pulpit read the marriage vow
while bridesmaid Violet peered from her bed.
Then suddenly, the spring—and you—were fled:
a wild rose on the pillow brushed my brow.

Those tears are pearls about my throat today.
My heart has found its resting place, and you,
your ears perhaps a thought less pointed, sing
the glories of your own hearth-fire—but stay—

let us not meet as other strangers do:
between us let it always be the spring.

II How Do I Love Thee?   1963

So many lights and shadows we have shared,
gone to the self-same water holes to drink;
woven as strong as spider-web the link
between us. Though on separate climbs we dared
and fell, whenever the fallen one despaired,
the other, waving frantic from the brink
the rope, so seeming frail, achieved, I think,
a little lift, knowing the other cared.

Two solitaries, half a world apart,
are held by Ariadne's thread, the stuff
of which the universe is woven. Heart
may hurt—yet stubborn lives refuse to blend,
communicating by a pulse. Enough!
The ball and chain would be the bitter end.

III How Do I Love Thee? 1970

It was a tourist trip through heaven and hell,
not stopping long at any station, or
knowing what was next, what sudden door
might open over the abyss, what bell
could summon flights of doves, what whisper tell
a secret buried fifty years or more:
you took my hand now—on the Stygian shore . . .

Unbirthday Card for a Distant Beloved   1971

It's true, like Everest, you're *there*—
but I am *here.*
The empty chair
beside the fire-place
yields no cheer
but makes a face.

Spirit is weak, but flesh is strong:
I eat alone and sleep alone,
converse mainly by telephone—
this has been going on too long.

Distance diminishes your charm
as: when the traffic light says **GO**
I bumble through the ice and snow
upheld by no supporting arm . . .

You ask, why must the man be you?
Your asking makes me wonder too.
Patience belongs with twenty-six
but heavenly day—at seventy-six?

Hindsight

Birthright

How can we look a baby in the eye
and say Welcome?
This wounded earth, one concrete cicatrix,
the wounded waters, masked with mud and oil,
the wounded air, hanging opaque,
alike reject us.

The birds who trusted in their brother man
are gone, the dodo and the auk
and now the robin.

So to the tender young
what heritage?

No Choice

A baby—a *baby?* A baby—oh no!
Baby, you will have to go.
There is no way to crowd you in . . .

Indeed it is a mortal sin—
a sin I must commit
and thereafter live with it.

Incommunicado
for Héloïse

It is not given us to see within
except by indirection.
Look through the window at the daytime moon
with a bird swaying on a branch across it;
people the world with images from caves;
be careful whom you tell.

The child in school looking through the window
ignores the writing on the board
in favor of the perching bird
or tries to mirror through unseeing eyes
what's taking shape within.

Ask him what he sees.
Will he say "Charlemagne on horseback"?
Or "The uncertainty principle"?
"Oh, nothing. I was just looking."

Hostages to Fortune
for Isadora

If the young mother dreamed
in how many ways she will fail her child
even the euphoria of childbirth
would hardly hold her up.

Early childhood is easy.
It is work we are built for;
the rewards are here and now—
a tickle, a giggle, a snuggle
a milky baby in the sun, learning to do—

Suddenly a teenager looking away—
what ever happened to Dick and Jane?

La Plus Belle Femme

Sarah, Rebecca, Rachel, Mary,
Jewish mothers all—
have I been a bad mother?

I nursed my children on ink and love:
inextricably mixed
that is what I had—
sometimes more ink than love.
What else could I have done?

That was what I had.

Blessing

Daughter, daughter, go in peace:
you can hardly come to harm
with your purse beneath your arm
and your whistle for police.
Gentle daughter, go in peace.

Tao

Did you ask the way?
There by the pool,
sun through barely stirring leaves,
wait.

Listen, look, and wait again.
It's a place within you,
needs no force to find.

The message awaits you there—
Bird, poem, prophecy—
your own.

Socrates 1970

Teacher, teacher, do you hear?
Teach me how to say it.
What I think you're asking, dear,
is about the nameless fear—
how can you allay it.

When you break a window, or
keep the college president
in his room and lock the door,
stop him working for the war,
action is your only vent.

We must listen when you say
in your crude and youthful way:
teacher, read your calendar!
You know how things used to be—
let us tell you how they are.

Irrelevant

The cemetery and the school
lie side by side across the fence:
this is indeed a learning tool
although perhaps a happenstance.

Almost April

Dear Teacher

    The blood in my veins was singing so loud
i couldn't hear another thing.
It isn't that I was naughty or proud
but there through the window blew the spring.

Teacher, teacher, don't you hear the tide?
Don't you feel the rhythmic beat?
Alive, alive! The world is wide—
how can I sit quiet in my seat?

Montessori School

To see a little child enjoy
coping with everybody's daily hardships
is to share that joy.

To lift that child-heavy table
and set it down without a bang
to walk that chalk line
carrying a glass of pink water
spilling just a drop
fitting ten cylinders into their holes—
joy for the child
joy for the observer.

There is no shadow on this joy
no ugliness of I am better than you—
it is the pure joy of welcoming the new person
into the world of those who can.

Late Sight

Love Story

Suddenly the gates flew open
and all that love flooded in.

Where was it hiding all those years?
Here it came, swirling in—
kisses, flowers, good wishes, a Duncan dance, a reading,
a record, a picture show—
a cartoon with three hats and nine muses—
a valentine pillow, a cake with ceramic box—
citations, a degree—
love—love—love—

The shadow hovers:
one daughter missing
hiding in hospital . . .
Will the tides of love reach her too
and sweep her back home?

City Delicatessen

The only way he could get any rest
was to work himself to death.

His wife got plenty of sympathy
and ran the store
another forty years.

A Little Late

Dear Charles

You say I have never made a poem for you
and it is true.
Nor have I made one for the maple tree that shaded
         our house
nor for my grandfather who saved my sanity a thousand
         times
by giggling with me in corners while our bosses conspired
to save the world from the forces of darkness—
why then did they wear black?

Poor grandma—poor mother—
trapped in a woman's world of impotence
without our power of laughter.

I could have been your mother
except I never slept with my brother.

You never saw my grandpa.
If they had planted a tree on his grave
as I hope they will on mine
it would have been fifteen years old when you were born.

You were a delight from the beginning
so full of response and understanding.
We had a common language
shared by none of our relatives.

Walking in Central Park, we passed the obelisk.
You said "That is where you told me about the death
        of Socrates
when I was five years old."
You were in college then;
the tie was real.

Now that I am old
and tired of making decisions
I lean too much on you
but I have never written a poem for you
unless this is one.

                              With love

Passover House
for John and Sooch Rannells

Why is this house different from every other house?
It is the house where everything works:
it is oriented to the sun,
the door knobs open the doors.
The cellar stairs respect us and are respectable,
the windows open and shut without complaining,
the faucets never have tantrums.
It was built with earthly love and rooted sense.

The Truth

I wish I dared to tell the truth:
no truth, no poetry.
Who asked to be a poet?

All right—here goes:
I HATE CARS
I want to run on flying feet
leap, climb, swim, ride lovely horses
wind in my hair, sun in my eyes.

KLOTZ!
Trifocals, shade hats, dentures, hearing aids, walking stick—
back ache, drag, tortoise pace
it's hot—it's cold—slippery streets
there's worse to come—
the dear sweet friends who drive me—
do I really love people
or just need them?

Reach Out

If I walk east at sunset
the shadow striding before fulfills my dreams
tall, slender—
long neck, long arms, long legs

Shadow! Stand up—be me!
Let the world see!

Don't Fence Me In

for John

Keeping an appointment
is like obeying the leash law.
Sometimes one does
out of sheer affection.

Even so it's perilous—
all those people out there
waiting to break your space bubble.
They mean no harm—
they only want you for their team.

Are You There?

To whom am I speaking?
To the ancestors who can no longer hear
let alone speak—
though I hear you all too clearly—
or to our descendants?

Here is what bothers me:
I can neither use your models
nor entirely discard them.
The hand-me-downs are too good to throw out
but they never quite fit.
Is that why I always feel like a clown?

Generation Gap

Why didn't I listen to my grandfather?
He was a forty-niner,
nineteen, penniless, fresh from Prague.
He hitch-hiked in covered wagons,
New York to California and back—
brought home a lump of gold as big as—
your thumb.
My nephew keeps it in his jewelry box;
all the gold Grandpa ever saw.

Think of the stories he must have told me . . .
he tottered when I ran to kiss him:
by spring he was dead.
I was fifteen and thinking about boys.

Did he stop off in Colorado?
I'll never know.

Far Sight

Prayer for Our Time 1941

Earth our mother and sun our father, suffer us to live.
We have not found our humanhood, we have betrayed
our knowing, we have been afraid,
we have not learned to give.

We have burned and stolen and flooded and killed;
plundered our good green planet, once designed
as an abundant home for humankind:
we know, and our knowing is unfulfilled.

Before our planetary home is blasted bare
may we remember: Man is one—on every brow is writ
"I am your brother." But we must be quit
of those who can not read, who will not share.

Sun our father, we have squandered morning light
on hideous deeds unworthy of the race of men;
give us your radiance on our brows again—
Sun our father, save us from this night.

The Next Step

To the ancient vine we cling
from the ancient vine we swing.

Mammal mother, walking free,
are you remembering the tree,
the baby clinging to your fur?
Do the buried memories stir?
With no help from tree or cave
now we must be quick and brave:
enemies in earth, in air,
in water, lurking everywhere.

Have we come so far in vain—
must we do it all again?

Another Chapter
(For *African Genesis*)

It seems that Cain the killer took a wife
and was our father in the ancient lineage
of killer apes.

Gone the good gorilla from the family tree
along with Abel who died virgin.

And Eden was in Africa where we emerged from animal
because and not in spite of our belligerence.

Oh Father Freud!
Grandfather Darwin, Uncle Marx—
who are we now?

Invocation at Delphi

It is true that when Phaëton lost control
of his father's horses
and the sun-chariot grazed Africa
burning the people brown,
only Phaëton died for his hubris.

They who would mount the sun today
are far from Phaëtons.
Oh, strike, Apollo,
before they cook us all.

Gonna Play on My Harp

Pull the petals of the battered daisies.
It will—it won't—it will—it won't—
Katy didn't—Katy did—
Tick tock—tick tock—tick tock—tick tock—
BOOM.
So it was a bomb.
Here I am in heaven with my harp
todo es musica
what a relief to be off the earth.

That's what you think
whereas on the contrary
here you sit darning socks
and the paper says
the commentator says
the newsdealer says
the milkman, the baby, the dentist, the garbage collector,
      all say

war
no more.

No more war?
Peace? On earth?
Good will? To men?
Then you really think you are in heaven?

The Woodchopper of Doorn
or
How History Repeats Itself

He was the most hated man of his time:
Kids used to say
"I don't care who kills the Kaiser."
But nobody killed him:
he died in bed.

Everything around him was breaking down.
The economy collapsed.
The coinage shrank
there were shortages, corruption, crime.
His family stuck with him
but nobody interviewed him
nobody photographed him
caricatured him—
nobody cared.

The emperor wore clothes
but nobody copied him
because after all
he was only an ex-emperor.

Late American

Permit me to repudiate the guilt
in which my forebears had no share.

I must accept the grandfather
who sent a stand-in to the Civil War
and stayed home to beget my mother;
the granduncle who ran the blockade,
the grandmother who trembled at Gene Debs—
their sins are on my head.

But praise be to Manitou
no ancestor of mine
betrayed the Indians.

Oil's Well

I —And John (D) is His Prophet (ca. 1926)

Omnipotent, oh Mar., beneath your red
sceptre bows every potentate—yea Pan,
Apollo, and that patient Son of Man
whose only crown was thorns—but he is dead—
did you not spew your scorn upon his head
at Rheims, and in his place crown Caliban
who gaily leads the pilgrim caravan
to your insatiate altar to be bled?

Till your cathedral be complete, oh Mars,
let every cross-roads hold a small red shrine
where motorists may stock with Socony
and pay their tithes to St. John the Divine
and ponder Israel's autonomy
and all the oil we'll win in future wars.

II Habeas Corpus (ca. 1929)

From their habit of suspicion
and their liking to confuse
agencies of Prohibition
once locked up the singing Muse.

Prison was depressing, dirty—
with no influential friend,
when the clock struck nineteen-thirty
poetry approached her end.
         And this
            was
               her swan song:

"Obsolete the miller's daughter
and the epic of the soil—
the remotest river's water
has a film of Mobiloil.

"Advertising panegyric
desecrates the rural scene
vanished is the lovely lyric
and the smell of gasoline

drowns the odor of the flowers
while the superheterodyne
and allied victorious powers
are supplanting me and mine."

III John the Baptist (ca. 1934)

Old John D
at ninety-three
eats crackers and milk
he can't take tea.

Under his windows the hundreds are marching
what are they chanting? He doesn't understand.
Yesterday the butler opened an upstairs window:
"Restore Rivera's murals!
Restore Rivera's murals!"
echoed from the streets.

Today the murals are returned to dust.
"Down with the vandals!"
comes through the window.
Close the window, James—
there is a draft on Mr. Rockefeller's neck.
"Down with the vandals!"
whistles in the chimney.
Oh James, we must have the chimneys cleaned.
How is the draft on your neck, Mr. Rockefeller?
Is it sharp like the Nazi knife?
You don't like the Nazis, Mr. R.—
very uncultured people—
they cut off heads with an axe
publicly.

So much more refined, don't you think,
to ship thugs into the far hills
to shoot down miners?
Didn't you forget to mention something, Mr. Rockefeller?
Ludlow—the name is Ludlow.
Did you remember to ask the gunmen if they were Baptists
before you hired them
before they shot the miners' wives?
Ludlow, Colorado, so long ago,
when you were a boy of seventy-two.

Old John D
is ninety-three
and he hasn't learned a single thing.
He thinks his little dimes
will cover up his crimes
so get his golden harp and let him sing.

But James—how did these persons get in?
Running over the rugs—my Oriental carpets.
Be careful of the crockery, gentlemen—
Mr. Rockefeller is a patron of the arts.

Oh Mr. Rockefeller—
why—where is he?
Who—that dried-up gut in the arm-chair?
That gut with the grasping hand?
Excuse me—I must have stepped on it—
I thought it was a mummy.

Old John D
made ninety-three—
that's par on this links
now he's ready for a hole in one—
one in a hole—
six feet under—

thank you, gentlemen.

The flowers in the hills of Ludlow are not so red this spring
the blue and yellow flowers have a chance at last.

Lorelei

The siren shrieks
wow wow wow wow
and streaks down the avenue.

People in the street
not in its path
pay no attention.
Tomorrow's paper will tell them who it was.

Epitaph for Ozymandias

Uneasy lies the head that plots against his brother
whose security blanket goes **BANG**—
poor Edgar Hoover
poor Howard Hughes
poor Ari Onassis—
their monument:
two stag skulls
with tangled horns
on sand.

My Lie

We beat the Nazis at a price:
something they had we caught.
Some moral spirochaete moves in us
poisoning the wells of human love.

The citizen soldier
one hand still on the plow
the military governor like a prep school principal
once our self-image
has given way to the unspeakables
our sons and brothers
who torture, burn, defoliate and orphan
these charming people in whose home we have no proper
          business
making them our "enemies."

Only in one way are we better than the Nazis:
we are ashamed
we lie.

Indispensable Man   A Montage

What did you see out there, John Glenn?
I looked at the Atlantic along the way I would follow;
we jumped the hurdles right on schedule,
the Atlas turned a corner in the sky—
I could look back the way I'd come
and see the entire state of Florida,
the Gulf of Mexico, and clear back to the Mississippi delta.

I found position by Orion and the Pleiades.
More than half a million feet above the clouds
I saw lightning in them like flashing bulbs.

I saw three sunsets and three dawns,
the stars subsiding near the horizon,
shining again before they set. The sun so bright
in the black sky, I had to filter it;
high in the sky it was bluish white.

Clouds hung solid over Central Africa
and the Pacific. The almost full moon
lit up the crisp, clear clouds.

The lighted city in Australia
was a warm and pleasant sight.

With the first ray of sunshine over the Pacific,
thousands of celestial fireflies,
greenish yellow, floated slowly by—
next time around I turned the capsule
and looked into the flow.
Were they snow-flakes from the capsule?

Heaven lies all about us;
what are we taking there?

You know who was there before you, John—
poor Laika—the moondog dead;
Able and Baker and Enos
Yuri and Titov
Al Shepard and Gus Grissom.

And who was with you there?
Cain and Abel
Eichmann and Einstein
your twenty thousand colleagues and Caroline
and everyone now living and to come
listening when you said:
I was flying this thing myself
and proving that a man is needed
on a normal day in space.

Note: Permission granted by *Life* magazine for the use of Col. Glenn's
        own words.

More Light

The Lesson for Today

God the bookkeeper is dead, fortunately,
and the quality of justice is not warm
so never ask
does What's-His-Name deserve my love?

Ask only
can I live without loving?

Have We?

Have we gone too far on the wrong road—can we no longer alter
      alter
our pattern? Have we faithfully promised to blast, and
      burrow, and perish?
Or may we draw the beautiful blue sky about us for shelter
and join hands around the earth that is still waiting, still
      willing, to nourish?

In Whose Footsteps?

Once the Carpenter, as late the President,
made a far journey to the Orient;
was it in search of wisdom that they went?

The wisdom of the Carpenter be done:
give love to children, healing, bread, to all
let Caesar have his coin, give God his own.

Who hears that voice? The three wise men are gone.
President, did you hear the Carpenter's clear call?

Leaden Lining

How often do I forget thee, Jerusalem?
(Treblinka, Theresienstadt, Auschwitz, Dachau)

Taking the clothes out of the wash
watching the children in the school yard across the street
or cloud shadows on the mountain's brow—
peace, peace, in my heart and in my garden,
war, anguish, the fighting face of brother man
the Hitler within—
hide them in the cellar of my soul.

What can I do?
Enjoy my last years
forgetting, forgetting.

Kol Nidrei

Open the Ark and take the Torah out.
I feel the generations walking through my heart.
Oh, save the Ark!
Our treasure is the Book.
Our warrior king was a sinner and a singer:
how we need his sins and songs today . . .
the God of mercy and loving kindness has forsaken us.
More than ever we are an endangered species.
They lock us in, chase us out, plot, encroach, threaten,
attack our home and our people.
Where are our leaders?

Oi, Oi, Oi

The Lord gave us the Ark of the Covenant
and all he asks in return
is the foreskins of our sons.
How explain this to the little man
who has just become a Jew
and wails in protest Oi Oi Oi Oi?

They Have Us in the Earth

The Lord said
Ye are a stubborn and stiff-necked people . . .

Be glad, my people.
Had we been flowers
we should have been crushed—
not some but all;
crushed by Babylonians, Persians, Romans, Goths, Huns,
        Turks and Huns again—
not to mention the Crusaders and other Christian neighbors,
our brothers over Jordan and cousins by the Nile.

We are as stubborn as seeds—
call us flowers, call us weeds;
we shall survive.

A Sort of Prayer during a Heat Wave and After Reading Martin Buber

All-Father (or All-Mother)
count it to me for good this day:
I have saved from the swimming-pool three lady-bugs
     and a moth;
the moth died, but not by drowning.
I escorted a hornet wrapped in cloth outdoors and released
     it unhurt,
killed a thousand seven hundred ninety-four ants
with a wet sponge instead of poison.
These mercies I did for myself as well as for them
     and Thee.

These evils have I done today:
held my temper three times and spilled it once,
spoken ill of my neighbor once against seven angers,
complained of the heat three times to others just as hot,
been sorry for myself,
been sorry for myself,
been sorry for myself.

Perhaps tomorrow may be better.